Loo

by Fernando Ruiz

illustrated by Larry Nolte

Printed in the United States of America

ISBN 0-15-317148-0 – Look at That

Ordering Options
ISBN 0-15-318574-0 (Package of 5)
ISBN 0-15-316985-0 (Grade 1 Package)

2 3 4 5 6 7 8 9 10 179 02 01 00

Look at this!

Pat is on it.

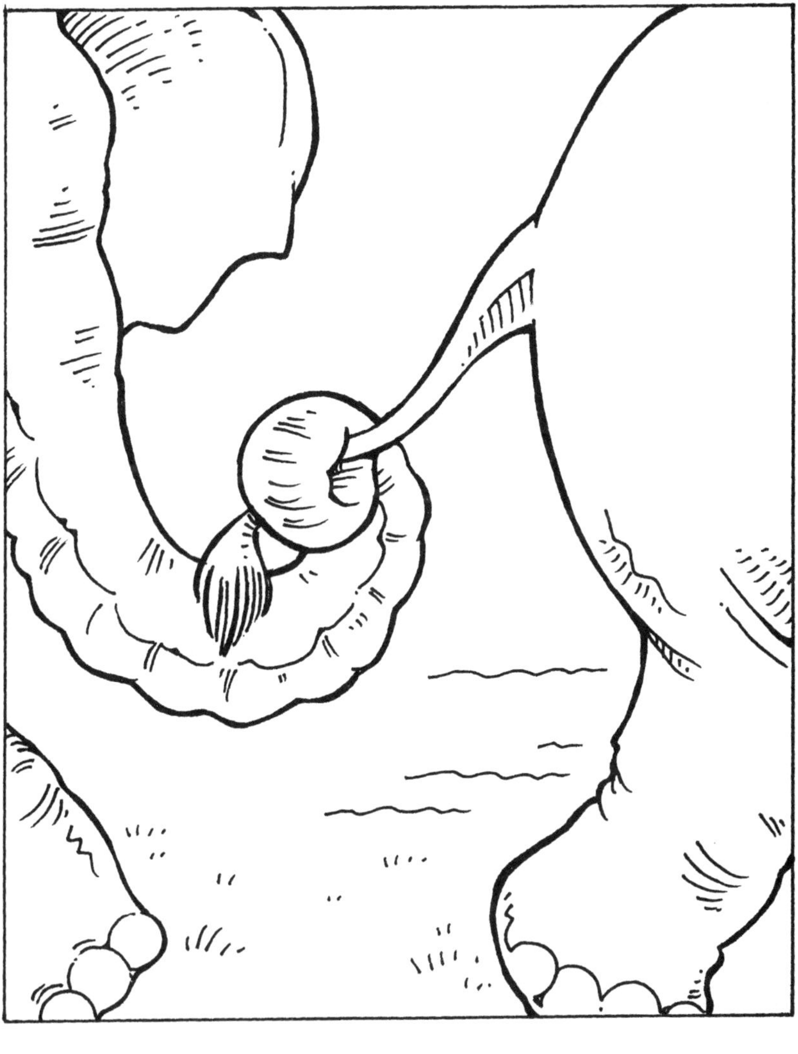

What will Pat see?

Pat sees Tim.

What will Tim do now?

Tim sits on it.

What will Tad do?

See what Tad did?

Teacher/Family Member

1, 2, 3!

Have your child read each sentence and then tell which happened first, next, and last in the story. (Turn the page to find the answers.)

Pat sees Tim.
Pat sees Tad.
Tim sits.

School-Home Connection

Listen to your child read *Look at That* to you. Then, ask whether he or she was surprised by the ending and why.

Word Count:	31	
Vocabulary Words:	on	do
	what	now
	will	this
	see	
Phonic Elements:	Short Vowel: /i/*i*	
	it	sits
	is	this
	Tim	will
	Consonant: /d/*d*	
	Tad	

TAKE-HOME BOOK

Open Doors

Use with "Come On, Dad" and "What Will Dad Do?"

Answers: First, Pat sees Tim. Next, Tim sits. Last, Pat sees Tad.